FRACTION MULTIPLICATION

USING LEGO® BRICKS

Dr. Shirley Disseler

COMPASS

Fraction Multiplication Using LEGO® Bricks — Student Edition

Brigantine Media/Compass Publishing
211 North Avenue
St. Johnsbury, Vermont 05819
Phone: 802-751-8802
Fax: 802-751-8804
E-mail: neil@brigantinemedia.com
Website: www.compasspublishing.org
www.brickmath.com

ORDERING INFORMATION
Quantity sales
Special discounts for schools are available for quantity purchases of physical books and digital downloads.
For information, contact Brigantine Media or visit www.brickmath.com.

Individual sales
Brigantine Media/Compass Publishing publications are available through most booksellers.
They can also be ordered directly from the publisher.
Phone: 802-751-8802 | Fax: 802-751-8804
www.compasspublishing.org
www.brickmath.com
978-1-9384067-2-0

CONTENTS

MULTIPLYING FRACTIONS USING ITERATION

Part 1

What is a fraction?

_____

_____

_____

Problem #1: ½ X ⁶⁄₈

1. Build a rectangular model of eighths using one 1x8 brick. Draw your model.

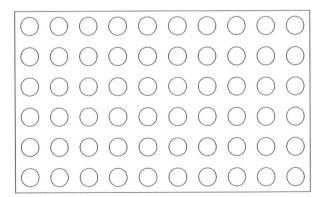

2. Stack a 1x6 brick on top of the 1x8 brick to show ⁶⁄₈.

Draw the 6x8 brick next to the 1x8 brick.

3. Model ½ x ⁶⁄₈ using iteration (the repeating process). To do this, use the 8 from the denominator of ⁶⁄₈ and the 2 from the denominator of ½. Iterate 8 by twos using eight 1x2 bricks by placing eight 1x2 bricks on the baseplate. How many studs are there in eight 1x2 bricks? _____

Draw your model.

4. Because the numerator of ½ is 1, cover one stud on each of the 6 bricks that model the numerator of ⁶⁄₈. How many studs are covering studs on the eight 1x2 bricks? _____

5. Model the product of ½ x ⁶⁄₈ using one 1x6 brick above one 1x16 brick. Write the number sentence for the problem. _____

Draw your model and explain your thinking.

_____

_____

6. To simplify your solution, locate bricks all of the same size that will cover the model of the product evenly for both the numerator and denominator. Which brick is it? _____

Count the number of **bricks** on the top that model the numerator _____ and the number of **bricks** on the bottom that model the denominator _____.

This shows the solution simplified to _____.

Draw your model and explain your thinking.

_____

_____

Problem #2: $\frac{2}{3}$ x $\frac{3}{4}$

1. Choose a brick that creates a rectangle that can be evenly divided into thirds. Cover that brick with smaller bricks that divide it evenly into thirds. Draw your model.

2. Find a brick that covers 2 of the thirds to model $\frac{2}{3}$. Draw that brick next to the drawing of the thirds model. Label your drawing.

3. Iterate the denominator of $\frac{3}{4}$. Use either 2x2 or 1x4 bricks. Iterate the 4-stud brick 3 times, based on the denominator of $\frac{2}{3}$.

4. Iterate the denominator of $\frac{2}{3}$ four times, based on the denominator of $\frac{3}{4}$, by iterating the 3-stud brick 4 times. How many studs there will be in the denominator of the solution?_____

5. How does this model show the commutative property of multiplication?

_____

_____

6. Using 1x2 bricks, cover 2 studs (the numerator of $\frac{2}{3}$) of each of 3 bricks (the numerator of $\frac{3}{4}$).

Place one brick that has 12 studs on the baseplate to show the denominator of the solution model.

7. Count the total number of studs in the numerator. _____

To model the solution, place a brick that shows that number of studs next to or stacked on top of a denominator.

8. Simply the solution by finding bricks that are the same and cover the entire model (top and bottom) without any studs left over. How many bricks are on the top? _____

How many are on the bottom? _____

This shows that the simplified solution is _____.

Draw and explain your process and label the drawing.

_____

_____

_____

Part 2

1. Can you multiply $\frac{1}{6} \times \frac{2}{3}$?

Use this process:

   a. Model sixths using one brick. Draw your model and explain it.
   b. Discover and explain the iteration process.
   c. Model the role of the denominators and numerators in the problem.
   d. Show and explain your solution in simplest form.
   e. Write a math sentence for your model.

2. Can you multiply ³⁄₄ x ²⁄₅?

    a. Find one brick to show fifths. Draw your model and explain it.
    b. Discover and explain the iteration process.
    c. Model the denominators and numerators in the problem.
    d. Show and explain your solution in simplest form.
    e. Write a math sentence for your model.

3. Can you multiply ³/₄ x ³/₈?

    a. Model eighths using bricks. Draw your model and explain your choice of bricks.
    b. Discover and explain the iteration process.
    c. Model the role of the denominators and numerators in the problem.
    d. Show and explain your solution in simplest form.
    e. Write a math sentence for your model.

Assessment:

1. Build a model to show ²/₃ x ¹/₂. Show the solution. Draw and explain your thinking.

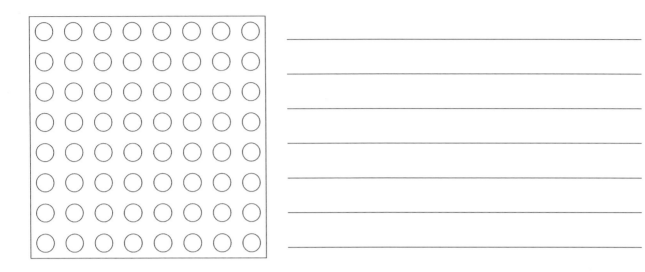

_____

_____

_____

_____

_____

_____

_____

2. Simplify the solution found in problem 1 (²/₃ x ¹/₂). Justify using a model.

3. What does ⁶/₈ x ¹/₂ mean?

_____

_____

_____

MULTIPLYING FRACTIONS BY WHOLE NUMBERS

Part 1

What does it mean to multiply whole numbers? What happens to the product as you multiply?

_____

_____

Does the product get larger or smaller when you multiply whole numbers?

_____

What happens when a fraction is multiplied by a whole number?

_____

Problem #1: John has 5 friends and they will each get $2/3$ of a sub sandwich. How many total sandwiches will they need to serve all 6 people?

1. Write a math sentence for this situation. _____

What does the math sentence mean?

_____

_____

2. Using bricks, model the math sentence. Draw and label your model. *Hint:* If you can, use the same color of 1x3 bricks to model the denominators since they are all the same. If you can, use different colors of 1x2 bricks to represent each person's part of the sandwich (the numerator).

3. In order to multiply a whole number by a fraction, the whole number must become a fraction. Count the number of studs on either a 2x3 brick or a 1x6 brick. How many studs are there on the brick? _____ This is the numerator.

How many bricks are there? _____ This is the denominator.

Each stud on the numerator represents the number of sets of 1x2 bricks needed to solve the problem. How many sets of 1x2 bricks are equivalent to 12? _____ Twelve studs represent the total number of studs in the 6 sets of $\frac{2}{3}$ that are needed.

4. To answer the problem (how many sandwiches they need to feed each person $\frac{2}{3}$ of a sandwich), find a brick with 3 studs that divides evenly into the total number of studs. Which brick will you use? _____

How many of these bricks fit perfectly into the model when aligning and comparing the bricks? _____ This represents the entire portion (new whole) that each person will get.

The solution is _____ sandwiches to serve all 6 people.

Build a model to show the solution. Draw and label it. Write the solution as a math sentence.

○ ○ ○ ○ ○ ○ ○ ○ ○ ○ ○ ○ ○ ○ ○ ○
○ ○ ○ ○ ○ ○ ○ ○ ○ ○ ○ ○ ○ ○ ○ ○
○ ○ ○ ○ ○ ○ ○ ○ ○ ○ ○ ○ ○ ○ ○ ○
○ ○ ○ ○ ○ ○ ○ ○ ○ ○ ○ ○ ○ ○ ○ ○
○ ○ ○ ○ ○ ○ ○ ○ ○ ○ ○ ○ ○ ○ ○ ○
○ ○ ○ ○ ○ ○ ○ ○ ○ ○ ○ ○ ○ ○ ○ ○
○ ○ ○ ○ ○ ○ ○ ○ ○ ○ ○ ○ ○ ○ ○ ○
○ ○ ○ ○ ○ ○ ○ ○ ○ ○ ○ ○ ○ ○ ○ ○

_____

_____

_____

Problem #2: Yesterday, the Donut Shop sold $\frac{5}{8}$ as many chocolate donuts as cinnamon donuts. If they sold 2 trays of cinnamon donuts, how many trays of chocolate donuts did they sell?

1. Identify the products in the problem and write the math sentence.

_____

What does the math sentence mean?

_____

Which factor is the multiplicand? _____

Which factor is the multiplier? _____

Hint: Multiplication of fractions follows the commutative property.

2. Build 2 sets of ⅝, using five 1x1 bricks to model 5. Draw the model and label the drawing.

_____

_____

_____

_____

_____

_____

_____

3. Join the bricks that represent the numerator. What do you notice about the numerator and denominator?

_____

4. What does the model show?

_____

Model the mixed number. Draw and label your model.

_____

_____

_____

_____

_____

5. Can you simplify the $^{2}/_{8}$? Model it with bricks, then draw your model solution and explain your thinking.

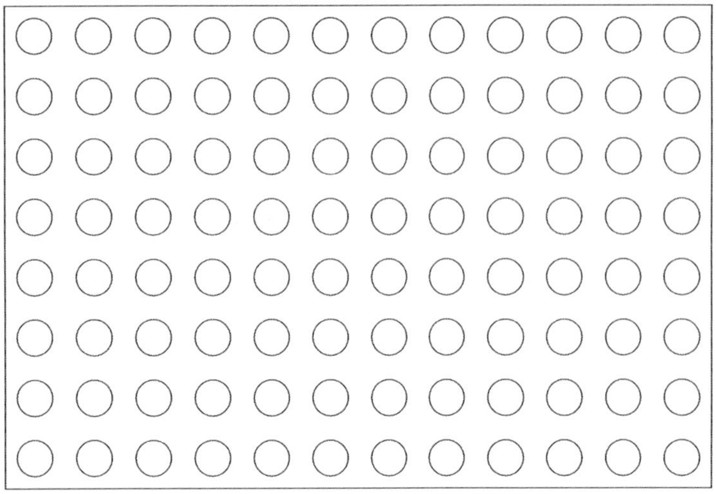

6. What is the final answer to the problem? ____________________

Problem #3: Build a model to show the process of multiplying $^{3}/_{4}$ x 3.

1. Write the math sentence. ____________________ What does it mean?

____

2. Model 3 sets of $^{3}/_{4}$ with bricks. Draw your model.

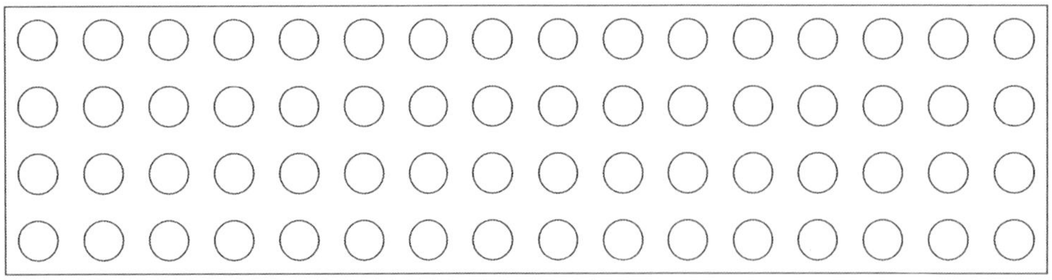

3. Join the numerator bricks together. Draw and label your model.

[brick model: 4 rows of studs]

4. Use bricks to model how many sets of the denominator are in the total number of the numerator. How many sets? _____ Draw your model.

[brick model: 4 rows of studs]

5. How many of the 9 studs are uncovered ? _____ What does this show?

_____

6. Draw the solution model, and explain what the model means. Write the math sentence and solution.

[brick model: 4 rows of studs]

_____

_____

_____

Part 2

1. Can you solve this problem?

The pizza shop sold ⅓ as many cheese pizzas as pepperoni pizzas on Friday. They sold 6 pepperoni pizzas. How many cheese pizzas did they sell? Model your solution, draw your models, and explain your solution in writing.

    Step 1: Write the math sentence for your problem.
    Step 2: Model the math sentence.
    Step 3: Build a model that shows how to find the numerator.
    Step 4: Model the denominator.
    Step 5: Show how many sets of the denominator are in the numerator.
    Step 6: Draw a model of your steps. Write a statement that explains your solution and label the drawing.

2. Can you solve this problem?

The school store sold 4 pencils on Friday. They sold $^3/_4$ as many pens as pencils. How many pens did they sell? Model your solution, draw your models, and explain your solution in writing.

   Step 1: Write the math sentence for your problem.
   Step 2: Model the math sentence.
   Step 3: Build a model that shows how to find the numerator.
   Step 4: Model the denominator.
   Step 5: Show how many sets of the denominator are in the numerator.
   Step 6: Draw a model of your steps. Write a statement that explains your solution and label the drawing.

3. Can you solve this problem? $\frac{1}{2}$ x 8

Show all the steps, draw your model, and label it. Write a math sentence and explain your solution using your model.

_____

_____

_____

4. Can you build a model that shows $\frac{3}{8}$ x 4? Draw your model. Prove it is a mixed number. Explain your thinking.

Challenge:
Simplify your solution.

_____

_____

_____

Assessment:

1. Find $\frac{2}{3}$ of 9. Build a model to prove your answer. Explain the model.

_____

_____

_____

2. What does 4 sets of $\frac{1}{2}$ look like as a multiplication problem? Build it and draw your solution model.

_____

_____

_____

3. Build a model to prove that the solution of a fractional multiplication problem will never be larger than the whole number in the problem. Explain your thinking.

_____

_____

_____

MULTIPLYING UNIT FRACTIONS BY FRACTIONS

Part 1

Make models of ½, ⅓, and ¼ with bricks. What are the similarities and differences between these three fractions?

_____

_____

_____

Define the term *unit fractions*.

_____

Which fraction is larger, ⅓ or ¼? How do you know?

_____

Problem #1: ½ x ⅔

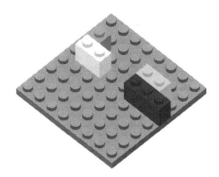

1. Model ½ and ⅔ and draw your model.

2. Explain the multiplication process.

_____

_____

_____

Model the process of solving the problem. Draw and label your model on the baseplate above.

3. The solution can be simplified. Draw the simplified solution and explain your thinking.

Problem #2: $\frac{1}{4}$ x $\frac{1}{2}$

1. Model each fraction and draw the model.

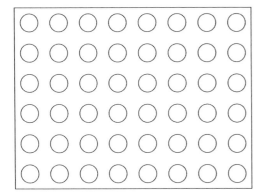

2. Explain the multiplication process.

_____

_____

_____

3. Model the solution. Draw and label the solution model on the baseplate above.

Problem #3: $\frac{1}{6}$ x $\frac{2}{3}$

1. Model each fraction and draw the models.

2. Explain the multiplication process.

_____

_____

_____

3. Model the process of solving the problem. Draw and label your model on the baseplate above.

4. The solution can be simplified. Model the simplified solution, draw it, and explain your thinking.

_____

_____

Part 2

1. Can you model ⅙ x ½? Draw your model and explain your solution.

_____

_____

2. Can you model $\frac{1}{2}$ x $\frac{3}{5}$? Draw your model and explain your solution.

_____

_____

_____

3. Can you model $\frac{1}{8}$ x $\frac{1}{2}$? Draw your model and explain your solution.

_____

_____

_____

Assessment

1. Build a model that uses repeated addition to show that ¾ is made up of 3 unit fractions. Draw and explain your model.

_____

_____

_____

2. Build a model to show the solution of ⅓ x ⅓. Draw and explain the model.

_____

_____

_____

3. What is a unit fraction?_____

_____

4. Build 3 examples of unit fractions.

UNDERSTANDING THE COMMUTATIVE PROPERTY

Part 1

What does it means to multiply whole numbers?

_____

Problem #1: ¹/₂ x 6 and 6 x ¹/₂

1. What do each of these problems mean?

¹/₂ x 6: _____

6 x ¹/₂: _____

2. Model ¹/₂ x 6 (¹/₂ of 6 wholes). Draw your model. Explain your thinking and how you arrived at the solution.

3. Model 6 x ½ (6 sets of ½). Draw your model. Explain your thinking and how you arrived at the solution.

_____

_____

_____

_____

_____

_____

_____

_____

Problem #2: Using ¼ x 8 and 8 x ¼, prove the commutative property of multiplication for fractions.

1. Work with a partner. One partner builds ¼ x 8 and the other partner builds 8 x ¼.

2. Draw both models and explain your thinking.

_____

_____

_____

Problem #3: Can you multiply two fractions by a whole number using the commutative property?

Answer before you model the problem:

_____

1. Model the problem $\frac{1}{2} \times \frac{1}{4} \times 8$ to show that you can rearrange the factors to make the solution easier. Choose a brick or bricks with 8 studs in total to represent the whole number.

2. Draw your model and explain your thinking.

_____
_____
_____
_____
_____
_____
_____
_____

Part 2

1. Can you prove that $\frac{2}{3}$ x 6 and 6 x $\frac{2}{3}$ are equal using the commutative property for multiplication?

Explain what the two expressions mean. How are they alike and how are they different?

_____

_____

Build both models, draw them, and justify your thinking.

$^2/_3$ x 6

6 x $^2/_3$

_____

_____

_____

2. Can you prove that $\frac{1}{3}$ x 3 and 3 x $\frac{1}{3}$ are equal using the commutative property of multiplication?

Explain what the two expressions mean. How are they alike and how are they different?

_____

_____

Build both models, draw them, and justify your thinking.

$\frac{1}{3}$ x 3

3 x $\frac{1}{3}$

_____

_____

_____

3. Can you prove that $\frac{1}{2}$ of 8 and 8 x $\frac{1}{2}$ are equal using the commutative property of multiplication?

Explain what the two expressions mean. How are they alike and how are they different?

_____

_____

Build both models, draw them, and justify your thinking.

$\frac{1}{2}$ x 8   8 x $\frac{1}{2}$

_____

_____

_____

Challenge:

Build a model to show the commutative property and solve: $\frac{2}{3}$ x 6 x $\frac{1}{2}$. Draw your models and explain your thinking.

Assessment:

1. Make two models that prove the commutative property of multiplication with fractions. Draw your models and explain your thinking.

_____

_____

_____

2. Using a model, solve $\frac{1}{4} \times 4 \times \frac{3}{4}$. Draw your solution. Explain how it is commutative.

_____

_____

_____

3. Explain how $\frac{1}{2}$ x 3 and 3 x $\frac{1}{2}$ are commutative. Build a model to prove your answer. Draw your model and label it.

_____

_____

_____

MULTIPLYING FRACTIONS USING AN AREA MODEL

Part 1

What is area?

_____

_____

_____

Problem #1: ¾ x ²/₃

1. Model each of the fractions, then draw your model and label the fractions.

2. Model the areas of 3 x 4 and 4 x 3 (the multiplication of the denominators of the two fractions). How many studs are in each model?_____ This number is the denominator of the solution.

Draw and label the vertical and horizontal models of the areas on the baseplate above.

3. Because the problem is ²/₃ of ³/₄, one model needs to show ²/₃ of the 3 x 4 model. Build this model using two 1x4 bricks vertically.

4. Because the problem is ²/₃ of ³/₄, the other model needs to show ³/₄ of the 4 x 3 model. Build that model using three 1x3 bricks horizontally.

These models demonstrate the difference between ²/₃ of 3 x 4, which is the vertical part of the solution, and ³/₄ of 4 x 3, which is the horizontal part of the solution.

5. Place the bricks that represent ²/₃ on top of the bricks that represent ³/₄.

How many studs on the 1x3 bricks are covered by the two 1x4 bricks? _____

Stack either six 1x1 bricks or one 2x3 brick on top to show the studs covered.

The studs covering the studs that are shared between the two models show the numerator of the solution. What is the numerator? _____

6. Model the solution to ³/₄ x ²/₃ using _____studs as the numerator and _____ studs as the denominator. Draw and label your model. Explain what the solution means.

_____

_____

_____

7. Simplify the solution using the largest brick(s) that fits on the numerator with no studs left over. Cover the entire model with these bricks. Draw and label your model. What is the simplified solution? _____

Problem #2: ½ x ⅔

1. Model each fraction. Draw your models and label the fractions.

2. Build an area model of each denominator. Count the studs to find the denominator of the solution fraction. What is the denominator of the solution fraction? _____

Draw and label the vertical and horizontal models of the denominator on the baseplate above.

3. Model ⅔ of the 3-brick model and ½ of the two-brick model.

4. Stack the horizontal model on top of the vertical model.

5. How many studs are covered? _____ Stack a brick on top of the covered studs to show the numerator.

6. Model the solution. Draw your model and label the fraction. This represents $\frac{2}{3}$ of $\frac{1}{2}$ of the whole of _____ studs.

7. Simplify the solution.

Part 2

1. Using an area model, can you show the solution for $^3/_8$ x $^2/_3$? Draw and label each step.

Step 1: Model $^3/_8$ and $^2/_3$. Draw your model.

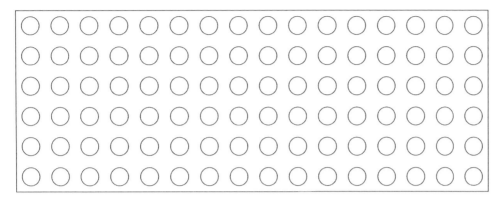

Step 2: Model 3 sets of 8 using three 1x8 bricks and 8 sets of 3 using eight 1x3 bricks, showing the denominator of 24. Draw your model.

Step 3: Model ²⁄₃ of the 3-brick model using two 1x8 bricks and 3/8 of the 8-brick model using three 1x3 bricks. Draw your model.

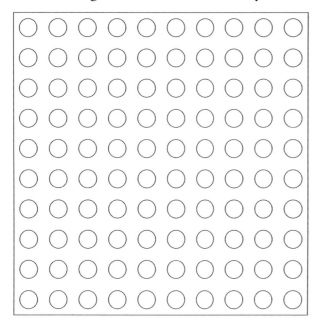

Step 4: Stack the 1x3 bricks on top of the 1x8 bricks. Draw your model.

Step 5: Count the number of studs covered. _____ Stack a 2x3 brick to show the numerator of _____. Draw your model.

Step 6: Model the solution. Draw your model.

Step 7: Simplify the solution by stacking bricks to cover both the numerator and denominator bricks. Draw your model.

What is the simplified solution? _____

2. Using an area model, can you solve $^3/_{10}$ x $^1/_2$? Draw and label each step.

Step 1: Model $^3/_{10}$ and $^1/_2$. Draw your model.

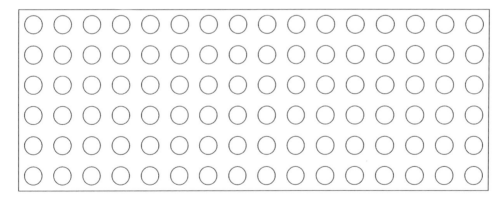

Step 2: Model the denominator of 20 using two 1x10 bricks and ten 1x2 bricks. Draw your model.

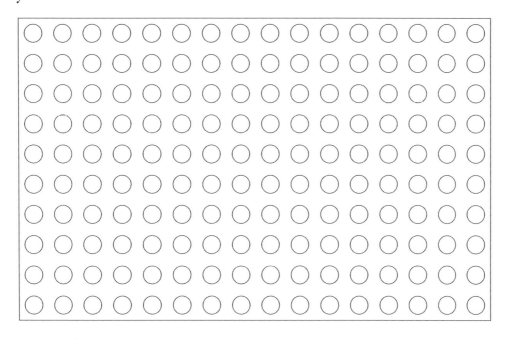

Step 3: Model ½ of the 2-brick model and ³/₁₀ of the 10-brick model. Draw your model.

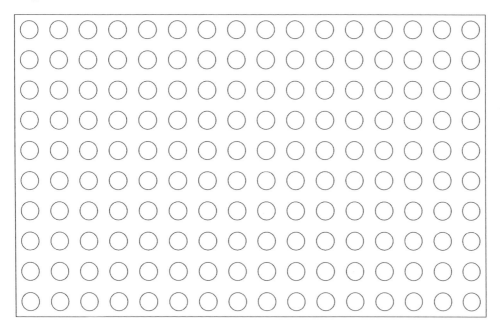

Step 4: Stack the 1x2 bricks on top of the one 1x10 brick and count the studs covered. How many studs are covered?_____ Draw your model.

Step 5: Stack a brick on top to show the numerator of _____. Draw your model.

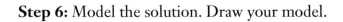

Step 6: Model the solution. Draw your model.

Assessment:

1. How can you find the area of a given space?

_____

_____

_____

2. Make an area model to show $\frac{2}{3}$ x $\frac{3}{4}$. Draw and explain your solution.

_____

_____

_____

3. Create a fraction multiplication problem that can be solved using an area model.

Write the steps for solving the problem. Model each step and the solution, and draw your models. Label all the steps.

_____

_____

_____

_____

_____

_____

_____

MULTIPLYING MIXED NUMBERS WITH LIKE DENOMINATORS

Part 1

Define the word *product* as it refers to a multiplication problem.

_____

_____

What do you think happens when a fraction is multiplied by a whole number?

_____

_____

Problem #1: Find the area of a rectangle whose sides measure 1½ x 2½. Build a model to show your solution. Compute the solution from your model.

Remember: When using bricks to model multiplication of mixed numbers with like denominators, the 1x1 brick will represent different amounts in each problem.

The denominator of the fraction will determine how many 1x1 bricks make 1 whole. For example, in the problem ½ x 2½, two 1x1 bricks (the denominator of the fraction ½, which is 2) are combined to create 1 whole. In the problem 2¼ x 3¾, the denominator of the fraction of the mixed numbers is 4, so four 1x1 bricks are needed to model 1 whole.

1. Place a 1x1 brick in the upper left corner of the baseplate. What does the 1x1 brick represent in this problem? _____

How many bricks does it take to make the whole? _____

2. How many 1x1 bricks are needed to represent $1\frac{1}{2}$ if each 1x1 brick represents $\frac{1}{2}$?_____
Place 1x1 bricks horizontally on the baseplate to model $1\frac{1}{2}$.

3. How many 1x1 bricks are needed to represent $2\frac{1}{2}$ if each 1x1 brick represents $\frac{1}{2}$? _____

Place more 1x1 bricks on your baseplate vertically to model $2\frac{1}{2}$. Note: Be careful! The corner 1x1 brick counts in both directions.

Draw both models.

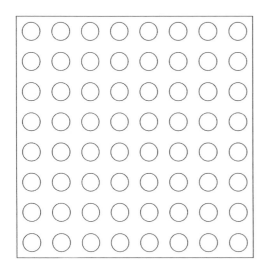

4. Fill in the rectangle area with another color of bricks. Note: Using a different color can help you visualize area, but it is not required.

Draw your model.

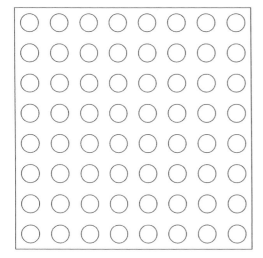

5. How many studs are there in total on your model? _____

6. Multiply the digit in the denominator of each fraction in the problem to find out which brick to use to cover the model. How many studs will this brick have? _____ This number is the denominator.

7. The denominator determines which bricks to use to simplify the improper fraction solution. To simplify, cover the model with bricks that have the number of studs to represent the denominator. Take the total number of studs_____ divided by the number of bricks used to cover the model_____. The bricks that cover the model represent the number of wholes in the solution.

How many studs are left that are not covered? _____ This number represents the numerator in the fractional part of the mixed number solution. Build the models, draw and label the parts of the model, and explain the solution.

_____

_____

_____

_____

_____

_____

_____

Problem #2: 3³/₄ x 2¹/₄

1. Place a 1x1 brick in the upper left corner of your baseplate. What does the 1x1 brick represent in this problem? _____ How do you know?

_____

_____

How many studs do you need to make 3 and ³/₄? _____

How many studs do you need to make 2 and ¹/₄? _____

2. Place studs horizontally on a baseplate to show the length of $3^{3}/_{4}$.

3. Place more studs vertically on the baseplate to show the width of $2^{1}/_{4}$.

4. Fill in the rectangle with bricks. Note: Using a different color of these bricks can help you visualize area, but it is not required.

5. Count the total number of studs in the model or use the idea of area (L x W) to multiply the number of studs in the length and width. How many studs are there in total? _____ This is the improper fraction's numerator.

6. Find the product of the digits in the denominators of the problem's fractions to give the denominator of the solution._____

What is the improper fraction solution (the total number of studs in the model over the denominator)? _____

7. The denominator determines which brick to use to simplify the improper fraction. Model the solution by covering the bricks with sets of _____ studs. What is the simplified solution? _____

Draw your models and explain the parts of the solution. Note: You will need to use a combination of bricks to model sets of 16 studs unless you have extra 2x8 bricks.

_____

_____

_____

Part 2

1. Can you find the area of 4½ x 2½ using a model? Draw your model and explain your solution. Follow the steps:

Step 1: Determine what a 1x1 brick represents in this problem. _____

Step 2: Build the horizontal (length) measure. _____ studs

Step 3: Build the vertical (width) measure. _____ studs

Step 4: Fill in the rectangle with bricks. Multiply the length studs by the width studs. _____

Step 5: Find the fractional part. _____

Step 6: Find the number of wholes by covering the area with sets of _____ studs. How many wholes are there? _____ Count the uncovered studs to find the fraction in the solution._____ Find the solution. _____

_____

_____

_____

_____

_____

_____

_____

_____

2. Can you find the area of $3\frac{3}{4}$ x $2\frac{3}{4}$ using a model? Draw your model and explain your solution. Follow the steps:

Step 1: Determine what a 1x1 brick represents in this problem. _____

Step 2: Build the horizontal (length) measure. _____ studs

Step 3: Build the vertical (width) measure. _____ studs

Step 4: Fill in the rectangle with bricks. Multiply the length studs by the width studs. _____

Step 5: Find the fractional part. _____

Step 6: Find the number of wholes by covering the area with sets of _____ studs. How many wholes are there? _____ Count the uncovered studs to find the fraction in the solution._____ Find the solution. _____

_____

_____

3. Can you find the area of $1\frac{1}{3}$ x $2\frac{2}{3}$ using a model? Draw your model and explain your solution in writing.

Step 1: Determine what a 1x1 brick represents in this problem. _____

Step 2: Build the horizontal (length) measure. _____ studs

Step 3: Build the vertical (width) measure. _____ studs

Step 4: Fill in the rectangle with bricks. Multiply the length studs by the width studs. _____

Step 5: Find the fractional part. _____

Step 6: Find the number of wholes by covering the area with sets of _____ studs. How many wholes are there? _____ Count the uncovered studs to find the fraction in the solution._____ Find the solution. _____

_____

_____

_____

_____

_____

_____

_____

_____

_____

_____

_____

_____

Assessment:

1. Build a model of $2\frac{1}{2}$. How many studs does the model have? Explain how you know.

_____

_____

_____

_____

_____

_____

2. Model the solution of $3\frac{1}{2}$ x $2\frac{1}{2}$. Draw your model and explain your thinking.

_____

_____

_____

_____

_____

_____

_____

3. Find the area of $1\frac{2}{3} \times 4\frac{1}{3}$ by building a model. Draw your model and explain your solution.

_____

_____

_____

FRACTION MULTIPLICATION
Student Assessment Chart

Name _____

Performance Skill	Not yet	With help	On target	Comments
I can model and explain the multiplication of unit fractions.				
I can show and tell what it means to multiply fractions using the correct vocabulary.				
I can model and explain the multiplication of a whole number by a fraction.				
I can model and explain how to find area using fraction multiplication.				
I can model and explain how to multiply mixed numbers.				
I can use the vocabulary for fraction multiplication appropriately.				

Printed in Great Britain
by Amazon

Towards a healthy future

Multiagency working in the management of invasive and life-saving procedures for children in family-based services

Richard Servian, Vicky Jones, Christine Lenehan and Steve Spires

for Shared Care Network

Shared Care Network

First published in Great Britain in 1998 by

The Policy Press
University of Bristol
Rodney Lodge
Grange Road
Bristol BS8 4EA
UK

Tel no +44 (0)117 973 8797
Fax no +44 (0)117 973 7308
E-mail tpp@bristol.ac.uk
http://www.bristol.ac.uk/Publications/TPP/

ISBN 1 86134 132 6

Front cover: photograph taken by Sue Mennear, posed by a model.

Richard Servian is Service Manager for Dudley Sharing Care. Previous publications include *Theorising empowerment* (The Policy Press, 1996). **Vicky Jones** is the Shared Care Network National Coordinator. She has edited a range of publications including *Stronger links*, *New horizons* (Shared care and the needs of people with autism) and *Quality counts*, a review of quality assurance methods. **Christine Lenehan** set up and now manages Barnardos Families Together, a family-based short-term care service operating in partnership with the London Borough of Tower Hamlets. Christine is one of the co-editors of the Barnardos good practice guide, *Supporting disabled children who need invasive clinical procedures* and *Sronger links* (a national good practice guide for shared care services). **Steve Spires** is Shared Care Coordinator for Essex Social Services. He is also a member of the Shared Care Network Management Committee.

The information included in this publication is as accurate as the authors have been able to establish and is intended to be useful and informative. However, neither the authors nor those involved with this publication are to be held responsible in any way for consequences arising from reliance upon, interpretation or use of the information within this publication.

Each individual must be responsible for themselves and approach with an enquiring mind. On this basis, further clarification may be sought or questions addressed via Shared Care Network at:

Shared Care Network
Norah Fry Research Centre
3 Priory Road
Bristol
BS8 1TX
Tel: 0117 928 9814
Fax: 0117 946 6553

Registered Charity No: 328572

Cover design by Qube Design Associates, Bristol.
Printed in Great Britain by Hobbs the Printers Ltd, Southampton.

Contents

Acknowledgements

Shared Care Network Policy Advisory Group

Gordina Appleton, County of Swansea

Vida Douglas, Shared Care Birmingham

Sarah Durrant, Cambridge Family Link

Vicky Jones, Shared Care Network National Coordinator

Christine Lenehan, Barnardos Families Together, Tower Hamlets

Peggy Maxwell, Newcastle upon Tyne Shared Care Service

Pat Verity, Deputy Director, National Foster Care Association

Steve Spires, Essex Shared Care

Richard Servian, Sharing Care, Dudley

We would like to express our thanks to the following for contributions, useful feedback and comments:

Dr Carol Robinson, Senior Research Fellow, Norah Fry Research Centre

Clare Richards, Services Manager, Sharing Care, York County Council

Alison Rhodes, Barnardos Policy and Development Unit

Jan Morrison, Project Leader, Newham Family Link

Emma Reid-Chalmers, Barrister and Shared Care Network Legal Advisor

Sue Burr OBE FRCN, Paediatric Nurse Advisor, Royal College of Nursing

Sarah Carr, Parent Advisor, Contact a Family

Jackie Thom, Nurse Specialist (Disability), Nottingham NHS Trust

Royal College of Nursing Children's Community Nurses Forum and Children with Disabilities Interest Group

Members of the National Executive Committee of the BAAF Medical Group

Celia Beckett, BAAF Medical Group Development Officer

Dr NPG Dave, Medical Centre, RAF Rheindahlen

Dr K Hassan, Specialist Registrar in Community Paediatrics

Summary and aim of these guidelines

Children with complex healthcare needs are a growing group using family-based short-term care services. However, many agencies have experienced difficulties and inconsistent advice regarding their responsibilities when placing these children. *Towards a healthy future* has been written to help agencies develop a local policy for the management of invasive and life-saving procedures administered to children using family-based short-term care and foster care services. Underpinning the whole document is the principle of children's rights and Chapter 1 highlights legislation supporting these rights.

Throughout the document a multiagency approach to devising local policies is advocated. The main issues for children, support carers and services are highlighted and guidance about the provision of any clinical treatment is offered. It also aims to clarify responsibilities for carrying out specific clinical procedures.

The guidance aims to be as flexible as possible to maximise opportunities for children, while identifying clear parameters in relation to when, how and by whom medication is given.

Chapter 1 explains why there has been an increase in the number of children with complex healthcare needs and describes the nature of family-based short-term care

services. It highlights the main difficulties services have experienced in placing this group of children and focuses on children's rights to receive services.

Chapter 2 outlines the legal framework, while Chapter 3 focuses on the practical aspects of agreeing a multiagency policy and focuses on issues that would need to be considered.

The appendices include a sample healthcare plan recommended by Barnardos and a series of sample forms adapted from those used by Dudley Social Services. These forms cover parental consent, guidance for the life-saving administration of medicines, records of training and a form which carers can use to record administration of medication.

An example of a protocol for children who require gastrostomy feeding is provided and an example of a multiagency group's approach to meeting the needs of children with complex healthcare needs is included in the final appendix as a model of good practice.

This guidance is the first of its kind specifically for family-based short-term care, and we would appreciate your comments in order to inform future developments or revisions. To facilitate this, a feedback form has been included at the end of the document (Appendix H).

A note about terminology

Throughout this document the following
terms are used:

Clinical procedures: refers to a procedure
which is carried out by non-medical staff.

Support carers or carers: refers to a carer
offering either short breaks or foster care to
children.

*Short-term breaks, family-based short-term care
and shared care:* all refer to an arrangement
where a disabled child has a series of short
pre-planned placements with a support
family or carer. These stays take place with
the same family/carer.

Parents: refers to the child's natural parent or
guardian.

Introduction and an outline of the main issues

Background

In recent years the number of children who have disabilities and conditions requiring clinical interventions has grown significantly. This is due, in part, to advances in medicine which mean that more children are surviving very premature birth and neonatal complications and those with degenerative conditions are living longer. Many of these children are now living at home, with their parents often carrying out routine clinical procedures. This group of children may require gastrostomy (feeding) tubes, suction, catheterisation, nebulisers or administration of rectal diazepam for the control of epilepsy and regular injections.

Many disabled children and their families use family-based short-term care services. Family-based short-term care schemes provide a support service to disabled children, adults and their families. They find another local family or individual who volunteers to have a child or adult stay with them on a regular basis. This could be anything from a few hours a week to a few days a month. Family-based short-term care services go by many names: for example, family link, shared care, home from home, families together, short breaks scheme or family-based respite scheme. On the whole, these schemes offer a similar service.

The general aims of any family-based short-term care service are to provide flexible short-term care within a family setting in order to:

- allow primary carers of disabled children to have a short break from caring;

- enable children to have the opportunity to widen their experiences and make new friends.

Shared care services benefit all the parties involved and the arrangement not only offers high quality care but is also cost-effective.

Children with complex healthcare needs and shared care – the current situation

As the number of children with complex healthcare needs grows, so too does the demand for shared care services. This is a popular service as parents know that their child will receive one-to-one attention in a familiar setting, unlike hospital or residential care where the staff change and there may be staff shortages. Lisa's son Steven, aged 5, spends about one weekend in five with support carers Jane and Ian.

"Jane takes on a lot of responsibility with Steven. He's on a minimum of eight different drugs a day, and it's always changing. And he very quickly becomes dehydrated, or seriously over-hydrated.

So, like me, Jane has to monitor this by constantly weighing him. But actually I feel more relaxed about handing him over to her than I have in the past when he's had respite care in hospital. She knows him so well, and I know the family watch him the whole time, which nurses on a busy ward just can't do."

Lisa and her family are typical of a growing number of users of shared care services. Shared Care Network has links with around 250 services and over the past year many of these services have contacted us regarding difficulties around placing children with complex healthcare needs.

The main issues

Initial research carried out by the Shared Care Network Policy Advisory Group highlighted the fact that most services were struggling with the following areas.

Training for support carers

If support carers are to administer any medication by invasive means or carry out a clinical procedure, it is essential that they have received training from an appropriate healthcare professional and are assessed as competent. There is currently a lack of clarity about the responsibility of health authorities to provide training for support carers. Practice differs widely around the country, but there are some examples of collaborative working between health and social services. (See Appendix G – extract from City of York Policy.)

This problem has remained unresolved due to a lack of both national guidelines and locally-developed policies. Where local authorities have developed guidance, it is sometimes inconsistent or driven by fear of litigation, which has led to the families concerned having problems in accessing the service.

Fear of litigation

Many local authorities are concerned about litigation against support carers should an allegation of negligence be made. The unclear legal situation has led to the failure or reluctance of various local authority legal departments to accept responsibility. However, support carers must be protected against allegations of negligence or abuse and children must be protected against actual negligence and potentially harmful practices.

"I felt very bad saying we couldn't offer short-term care to Kelly. Her parents were desperate for a break. But our health authority hasn't sorted out the insurance issue for care staff giving rectal diazepam; …. It seems ridiculous that children who most need our service don't get it, not because they are too difficult but because no one can sort out the 'risk' over who administers drugs…." (Carer, cited in Russell, 1996, p 48)

It is apparent that some local authorities have resolved these difficulties by refusing children with complex healthcare needs access to the service. However, in most cases, a short break within a family setting is more appropriate than a hospital placement.

Children's rights and access to services

Underpinning this document is the principle of children's rights. There are three main areas of legislation which reinforce the fact that children have a right not only to equality of access to services, but access to the services which are best suited to their needs. The relevant legislation includes the 1989 UN Convention on the Rights of the Child, the 1995 Disability Discrimination Act and the 1989 Children Act (1995 Children [Scotland] Act, 1995 Northern Ireland Children Order).

Local authorities who fail to implement the necessary procedures to enable children access to shared care services could be considered as denying children their rights as set out in the UN Convention on the Rights of the Child (1989).

The 1995 Disability Discrimination Act states that disabled people must not be discriminated against by those providing goods, facilities or services. Again, a failure by local authorities to provide a service to this group of children could be considered to be discriminatory.

Under the Children Act legislation, local authorities have a statutory responsibility to provide a range of services and support for disabled children and their families which are designed to minimise the effects of disability and give them the opportunity to lead lives which are 'as normal as possible'. A key principle of the legislation is that children should be brought up in their own families and families should be supported to do this. Provision of short-term care within hospital settings is not only unsatisfactory for children but usually an inappropriate use of hospital services.

In fact, the Department of Health first 'cardinal principle' as outlined in *The welfare of children and young people in hospital* (1991) is that "children should not be admitted to hospital unless the care they require cannot be provided in another setting".

The fourth cardinal principle is also applicable, that is, that "children should be discharged from hospital as soon as socially and clinically appropriate and full support provided for home or day care". The present government continues to support these principles (DoH, 1997).

It is clear that both health and social services need to work together to effectively meet the needs of this group of children and comply with the legislation and the recommendations made by the Health Committee. The government response to the reports of the Health Select Committee mentioned above highlights further the need for multiagency collaboration:

We are committed to reducing the current fragmentation of services between social services, health and education agencies ... there is a need for a new spirit of co-operation between the agencies which, together provide services for children. It is important that the needs of the child or young person are met, and that disagreements about who provides a particular service or item of equipment should not disrupt the care of the child. (DoH, 1997, p 12)

Towards a healthy future encapsulates many of the Health Committee's recommendations for multiagency working. The document takes as its starting point the principle of children's rights. It aims to clarify responsibilities and outline the issues and procedures that should be included in a local policy.

The legal framework

This chapter looks specifically at the types of clinical procedures support carers might be expected to carry out in addition to the general administration of medicines. The implications of carrying out these procedures are outlined, based on legal advice given to Dudley Social Services.

What sort of healthcare and clinical procedures do we mean?

These procedures are defined as actions necessary to promote or maintain health. They might be undertaken as part of a child's routine care or in an emergency.

Examples of invasive procedures include: feeding through gastrostomy or nasogastric tube; suction; catheterisation; administration of rectal diazepam for the control of epilepsy; medication by injection; oxygen administration; or assistance with nebulisers. Parents will generally have been provided with training by healthcare professionals to carry out these procedures at home.

There are two main sets of circumstances in which administration may be necessary:

- long-term illness or chronic conditions where medication is administered and/or procedures are carried out on a routine basis, for example, for feeding;

- emergency situations which may arise from time to time because of a long-term condition, for example, epilepsy, asthma.

What are the legal implications of support carers providing these procedures?

Carers have expressed concerns that they may become involved in procedures with which they are not qualified to deal, but if they do not do something the person they are supporting may be at risk. As mentioned earlier, the uncertainty around the legal situation has led many local authorities to withdraw services to this group of children.

The following advice regarding the legal situation was given to Dudley Social Services. There are three main legal issues to be considered: trespass, necessity and duty of care.

Trespass: any intrusive procedure involves the legal tort of trespass to the person and requires either proper informed consent or specific justification. The policy of law is always likely to discourage unqualified people from carrying out medical treatment unless it is essential and unavoidable. In such circumstances much depends on the state of medical advice and the needs and requirements of the individual client.

Necessity: a defence against a claim of assault is that the treatment was applied through necessity. Not only must there be necessity to act when it is not practicable to communicate with the assisted person but also the action must be such as a 'reasonable person' would take, acting in the best interests of the assisted person. Intervention cannot be justified when another more appropriate person is available and willing to act, nor can it be justified when it is contrary to the known wishes of the assisted person, to the extent that they are capable of rationally forming such a wish.

The starting point is that the treatment must be lawful in the first place. In law, every person is entitled to have their body left alone and any interference will be unlawful unless it is physical contact generally acceptable in the ordinary conduct of everyday life.

Duty of care: this is subject to the common law principle of the need to preserve life, health and well-being. If carers have undertaken the responsibility to provide care and protection, they cannot simply stand by and do nothing in the knowledge that life threatening consequences may follow. The actual obligation will depend on the situation – it may be to call for medical assistance or it may be to apply medical treatment, where more appropriate personnel or advice is not present, or is unlikely to be present in time to save the person from harm.

A duty of care is imposed on anyone who takes on the care of a 'helpless or infirm' person. If the duty of care is breached by a failure to take proper care, there can be civil liability in negligence.

Giving treatment in non-urgent situations

The individual decision whether to give medical treatment has to be a medical judgement. If the person responding to a medical need does not have medical qualifications or relevant training then no competent body of medical opinion would be likely to regard it as sensible for that person to intervene.

Non-urgent treatment must be governed by approval by medically-trained personnel. This can be given:

- on the spot by qualified personnel;

- by general approval to cover a type of situation;

- specific approval in an individual instance.

The nature of the approval should be based on a protocol between the relevant social services department, and the health authority or trust. The approval document should outline the minimum standards expected of the carer and other non-medical or nursing staff, and which conditions and situations they are to cover.

Giving treatment in emergencies

The general principles are the same as for non-urgent situations, although the duty of care becomes even more important in an emergency situation.

Liability

If the carer is an employee

If the caring individual does nothing where there is a duty to ensure that the person supported receives medical attention then they may be civilly and criminally liable. Employees acting under the direction of their employers and in good faith should be exempt from civil proceedings, although their employers will not be. Employees, however, will not be exempt from criminal action.

If an authority's policy prevents its non-medically-trained personnel from intervening where a more appropriate person is not available, then the authority could be subject to civil proceedings and the individuals following such a policy to criminal proceedings if someone is injured or dies an avoidable death. This means that a policy that says certain individuals can never intervene is probably unlawful. This has to be balanced by the need to act only with informed consent or justification.

If the carer is a foster/short-term carer

Foster carers have been deemed by the Court of Appeal (*S v Walsall MBC 1985*) not to be agents of the local authority so are solely liable in a successful action for negligence. They are expected to exercise the same level of prudence as a reasonable parent. So, if foster carers are following an authority policy not to intervene, and injury or death results, then they, not the authority setting the policy, are likely to be liable.

Insurance

Local authorities have a responsibility to protect carers against claims for alleged negligence and at the same time to protect children from actual negligence. This means taking all reasonable steps to ensure that children receive the best possible care and that carers are properly trained and equipped to care for them. Services should ensure that carers have suitable insurance cover and should check their own public indemnity insurance. (See Chapter 3 for details of National Foster Care Association insurance.) If the guidelines outlined below are followed, the risks to both children and carers will be minimised.

Nurses who are approved short-term carers

If a support carer is also a qualified nurse or other health professional then it is the responsibility of the scheme to ensure that the carer checks their own indemnity with the body with whom they are registered.

In summary, the legal advice is that each expected situation should be governed by detailed written guidance drawn up by relevant health and local authority departments.

Agreeing a local policy

This chapter focuses on the practical aspects of agreeing a joint policy and highlights some of the issues a multiagency group might need to address.

Working with the health authority

For children to receive the best possible care, social services and health authorities need to work together. Shared Care is part of a range of services a child may receive and the needs of the child should be central and transcend agency boundaries. Joint working, however, has not always happened because of confusion around responsibility and liability, but a report from the House of Commons Health Committee, session 1996-97, 'Health services for children in the community: home and school', is clear in its recommendations.

It is not acceptable that any health professional should be prevented from giving training to other carers through fear of litigation or through confusion as to his or her legal liability. We recommend that the DoH issue clarification to health authorities and trusts on this matter. In particular we believe that it should be made clear that the training of parents and non parent carers by health care professionals is an important part of the work of the NHS. Those who are in it should be indemnified accordingly, either by the employing NHS body or (possibly more cost effectively) by the NHS centrally

(which could either self insure or take out actual insurance).

We also recommend that the DoH should examine and clarify the legal position of non parent carers, especially formal carers such as teachers and those providing respite care. As this kind of formal care can greatly reduce the burden on the NHS, by reducing the need for care to be given by health professionals, it does not seem intrinsically unreasonable that the NHS should bear the cost of indemnifying these individuals. (DoH, 1997, p 25)

In some areas health authorities and social services departments have worked together very successfully using a multiagency model to agree a joint protocol (Appendix G). A working group could include:

- paediatricians
- community nurse
- community paediatric nurse
- parent or representative of an appropriate parents' group
- relevant voluntary organisation
- legal representation
- representatives from the relevant services.

It may also be judicious to include both social services and health registration officers since they often have a view about what is permissible and have considerable power and influence. In some cases it may also be useful to involve a senior education officer.

Once a protocol has been drawn up, approval should be sought from the following parties at the most senior level:

- community paediatric nurses
- community nurses
- paediatric home carers
- home carers
- hospital consultants
- relevant voluntary organisation
- legal representatives
- parents/carers.

While not essential, it may be prudent to also consult:

- registration officers from social services
- registration officers from health
- education – executive/director.

Shared Care is part of a range of services that children may receive and any policy should reflect this – placing the child firmly at the centre and ensuring that it applies in all settings.

What should be included in the policy?

Some of the issues that need to be considered would include:

- what procedures support carers can carry out;
- drawing up a healthcare plan;
- parental and child's consent;
- obtaining information about the child's specific needs;
- information for carers;
- training for support carers;

- recording administration of medication;
- monitoring and review;
- what happens if a child dies;
- resource issues;
- insurance and indemnity.

These will each be considered in turn.

What sort of procedures can support carers carry out?

The sort of procedures which support carers could carry out should be agreed jointly by health and social services. The Royal College of Nursing (RCN) suggest that under certain conditions various tasks could be delegated. The conditions are that the carer has received appropriate training specific to an individual child, and that the carer's ability is regularly assessed. The date the assessment is due should be documented and the health professional responsible for carrying out the assessment clearly stated.

The tasks the RCN deems **appropriate** to carry out under these conditions are:

- administration of prescribed medicine via a naso-gastric tube;
- feeding through a nasogastric or gastrostomy tube;
- tracheostomy suction and emergency change of tracheostomy tube;
- injections (intramuscular or subcutaneous) with a preassembled pre-dose loaded syringe;
- intermittent catheterisation and catheter care;
- rectal medication;
- emergency treatments;
- assistance with inhalers, insufflation cartridges and nebulisers;
- assistance with oxygen administration;

- basic life support/resuscitation;
- administration of prescribed oral medication.

The RCN suggest that the following tasks should be **prohibited**:

- administering non-prescribed medicine (staff or carers may not know whether the medication may react with other medication taken);
- giving injections involving assembling syringes, administering intravenously, or controlled drugs;
- programming of syringe drivers;
- filling of oxygen cylinders (this is prohibited under Section 9 and 10 of the Medicines Act which states that "this can only be carried out by operators holding a manufacturers Licence").

Where non-prescribed medicines are needed (such as Calpol or cough mixture), they can be prescribed by the child's doctor. This would help ensure safe administration by carers and avoid any potentially harmful side-effects which might occur.

Healthcare plans

Every child who is looked after by the local authority, for however long or short a time, must have a healthcare plan. Although it is not a statutory obligation to have a healthcare plan for children who are not accommodated (ie, who have day care only), it is good practice to do so. The child should be involved in compiling their own plan if possible.

The plan should include:

- the child's specific healthcare needs and details of warning signs for particular conditions;
- details of the treatment;

- areas of concern where health promotion is appropriate (eg, sexual health, illicit use of drugs, dental health, hygiene, etc);
- any clinical procedure which needs to be carried out, by whom, under what conditions, when and how;
- what expectations there are for carer/worker involvement;
- which key health professionals are to be involved;
- what risk factors there may be;
- training needs, including who will need to be trained and who will provide the training;
- where more information may be obtained;
- a description of what constitutes an emergency, what action should be taken and by whom;
- consent to treatment.

The healthcare plan should be agreed with health, social services, the voluntary sector (if appropriate), the parents and, where appropriate, the young person and signed by all parties. Plans should be reviewed at least annually, or more frequently if the situation changes. The date the review is due should be stated on the plan. A sample healthcare plan recommended by Barnardos is included in Appendix A.

Obtaining parental and child's consent

Prior written parental consent should be obtained for any administration of medicines or clinical procedure and should be included in the short-term placement agreement. Appendix B is an example of a parental consent form for the general administration of medicine. It should be used to specify which medications and treatments carers may give, and how they are given. It also gives choices to carers in deciding how to take responsibility for medication. For example, they may decide just to store medicines for others, such as community nurses, to use rather than give medication directly. If carers or staff are unwilling to take responsibility for treatments then alternative arrangements will need to be made.

This consent form will need to be supported by a letter from the doctor or consultant. The parent or service user will need to ask the doctor to provide this at the time prescriptions are made or renewed. This will allow carers and staff to demonstrate that they are following medical guidance.

Although the consent form outlined in Appendix B is for the general administration of medicines, it could easily be adapted to include specific clinical procedures and suggestions are made for possible adaptations.

The wishes and feelings of children, and consent

Wishes and feelings: where possible the wishes and feelings of the child should also be ascertained using communication methods appropriate to the child. With children with limited communication skills, this means that alternative methods of communication should be attempted.

Consent: the consent of informed children about medical interventions should be respected, although whether the child is of sufficient maturity to understand the consequences of this consent can be taken into account by parents. An essential principle is the need to respect the individual. In law, any parental power to act for the child is lost if it is exercised against the interests of the child. For example, if parents, carers and key workers are of the view that a child is of sufficient age and maturity to self-administer varied amounts of medicines, as with perhaps the use of asthma inhalers, then this should be

encouraged, subject to medical advice and agreement with parents.

Obtaining information about the child's specific needs

The agency needs to collate as much information as possible about the child's specific needs in order to pass this on to carers. Parents will have the most detailed knowledge about their child's condition and they will be responsible for giving the service sufficient information about their child's healthcare needs.

Information should also be obtained from the child's doctor or other health professionals and this should include details of:

- the child's medical condition;
- medication including dose, method of administration, and possible side-effects;
- other treatments in place;
- special dietary requirements;
- the child's method of communication.

Any exchange of information between doctors or other health professionals and the agency should be with the consent of the child or the parent/guardian. Agencies should obtain written consent from parents to enable the doctor to release confidential information about the child.

What information does the service need to give to carers?

In order to provide the best possible care to children, support carers need as much detailed information about the child's specific needs as possible. Using the information from the health assessment and the healthcare plan, detailed profiles and procedures can be drawn up. Support carers should treat this information with the utmost confidentiality and share it only with those who need it.

In summary, carers should be provided with easily understandable written carers' packs (in the carer's first language) which, in addition to the standard entries, include:

- a copy of the child's health assessment form;

- as much background information on the child's condition as possible;

- information about specific clinical issues for the individual child;

- signed parental consent form;

- record of administration of medication (carers should record all medication given – this should include date, time, name of medication and dose, and any reaction);

- procedure for seeking advice in a non-emergency situation;

- emergency contacts including: doctor, paediatric home care team, agency, parent plus one other emergency contact (friend or relative);

- a guide to how they should act in particular circumstances or emergencies.

Appendix C(i) is an example of a protocol for emergency procedures used by Dudley Social Services. This form is used to supply full details of an individual's medical conditions which are likely to need support in emergency circumstances. The form should detail the exact circumstances in which emergency treatment should be undertaken and should be signed by an appropriate medical officer. Given the time-consuming nature of preparing a form, the information could be prepared by informed others, for instance, by a community nurse, and confirmed by an appropriate medical officer. There is likely to be a need to discuss financial support for doctors undertaking this work.

The form outlined in Appendix C(i) should also be used where other sudden medical situations arise, such as allergies. It should be completed in such a way as to help carers prepare for an emergency. This will include information on danger signs, and trigger situations as well as things to avoid. For instance, in the case of allergic reactions, it will be important to note items which may cause allergies and note any necessary precautions.

An edited example of the form, for a child with severe allergies, is included in Appendix C(ii). The length of this reflects the needs of the child concerned and should not necessarily be seen as an indicator of the length of all similar forms.

Note: Medical advisors suggest that carers are recommended Hepatitis B immunisation and made aware of any other infection risk either they or the child faces and appropriate training is provided.

Training for support carers

Training for family-based carers should be provided at three levels: preparation, basic and specific training.

Preparation training

The purpose of this training is to give carers a basic understanding of childcare issues. It forms part of the approval process. This does not, however, constitute sufficient training for carers who may look after children with complex healthcare needs.

Basic training

Once carers have been approved they should be provided with mandatory training in the following areas:

- child health awareness, for example, signs

and symptoms of illness;

• administration of medication;

• First Aid and Resuscitation – it is recommended that this is given in the first year and then updated every three years;

• Moving and Handling (mandatory where carers are required to do this).

Courses may be provided by organisations such as the Red Cross, St John's Ambulance, British Epilepsy Association, or the health authority professionals, including physiotherapists and community pharmacists.

Training departments may wish to consider arranging authority-wide training programmes in these areas. In this situation services could purchase places for their staff and carers as required.

Note that these requirements are in addition to the usual training support carers would be expected to receive. Child protection training and training around intimate care should contain specific reference to children with complex healthcare needs.

Specific training

This should be part of any agreement for a child who requires invasive clinical treatment. All carers or staff must be trained by a healthcare professional in the administration of invasive clinical treatment and any possible side-effects. The training should be specific to individual children. If a support carer offers breaks to more than one child with complex healthcare needs, it is not sufficient to receive training for one child and transfer the skills for a task to the second child. General training on procedures is not sufficient: support carers should receive specific training for each individual child.

Parents need to be involved in this training since they will have a greater understanding of the particular needs of their child. There

may be helpful tips which the parent can give to carers such as "Tony prefers his red teddy to be beside him when his gastrostomy feed is given". This sort of information not only enhances the quality of care for the child but also reassures the parents that their child's care will incorporate their likes and dislikes. This information should be documented and included in the protocols given to carers.

Although the involvement of parents in training is important, training by the parent only is insufficient. Parents may be experts in their child's needs, but they have not been trained to teach others how to carry out clinical procedures.

Who should provide the training?

The following are suggested guidelines.

Training by a community pharmacist, named nurse

• Administering prescribed medicine orally. Carers must be fully aware of the contra-indications, possible side-effects and subsequent action to be taken. While the pharmacist could give information as to when a drug is given and side-effects, training in the actual administration of the drug should involve the child's parent and named nurse.

Training by doctor, named nurse, pharmacist or professional specified in the healthcare plan

• Administering controlled drugs orally.

Training by the child's doctor, community nurse or paediatric nurse

• Rectal medicine/emergency treatments. Training must include advice on the circumstances in which carers must act and pointers to look for. There should be written guidance in relation to the individual. When recording action taken, carers should note symptoms or signs which prompted their intervention as well as medication given.

- Assistance with oxygen administration. Support carers must understand the signs and symptoms requiring oxygen administration; the rate of flow; % mask; litres per minute; sign/symptoms of overdose; how to change cylinder head; safety precautions regarding storage and use of cylinders; recording systems as required.

Training by the nurse specified in the healthcare plan

- Administering prescribed medication via a nasogastric tube.

- Injections (intramuscular or subcutaneous) with a pre-assembled pre-dose loaded syringe.

- Assistance with inhalers, insufflation cartridges and nebulisers: training by the nurse with responsibility for the child or asthma nurse. Written guidance will be required on the number of inhalations and what to do if there is no effect.

The specific training that will be arranged should be outlined in the *Short term/Foster Placement Agreement* with carers. The *Foster Care Agreement* between the carer and the agency could include an agreement from the health authority to provide training and these should reflect the agreed agency protocols.

All training must be recorded, with the dates given, areas covered and the qualifications of the trainer. Appendix D(i) contains a sample record of training. The purpose of this form is to enable a healthcare professional to identify who has been trained for which procedure and for whom the treatment will be available. It should also state that the person trained has satisfactorily learnt the procedure.

The carer must also sign to say that they understand the procedures and the effects of

any medication. It is important to ensure that the carer is confident to carry out the procedures.

No child should be looked after by a carer until this training has been provided. This training will need to be updated on a regular basis. All information must be dated and include the review date. A form is attached in Appendix D(ii) which should be completed by healthcare professionals for updates and new methods. The frequency at which training should be updated must be agreed with the health authority concerned.

Where possible it may be helpful to link the child with a carer who lives in the same health authority as the child in order to overcome any difficulties in accessing emergency health services (eg, doctor).

In addition to the training, written information on the procedure in question should be given to the carers for reference and must be in the carer's first language. Multiagency groups may need to prepare protocols for a range of specific health conditions. The Nutritional Care Team at the Children's Hospital in Ladywood, Birmingham, have produced some useful general guidelines on tube feeding for parents and children (1994a; 1994b).

Appendix F is an example of a step-by-step guide to gastrostomy feeding drawn up by the nursing coordinator attached to the Sharing Care scheme in York. This general procedure would need to be adapted to meet each child's individual needs.

Recording medication

All medication that is administered should be recorded (see Appendix E, a suggested form for recording both regular medication and emergency treatments).

Support carers should receive training on how to observe and record information. In families where carers are unable to write, other methods could be encouraged, for example, use of tape recorders and medication dispensers to ensure the correct dosage has been administered each day.

Monitoring and review

The child's clinical needs and the ability of staff and carers to meet these needs must be reviewed on a regular basis. For those services providing short-term breaks, such systems should already be in place, that is:

- *The Child Care Review* – must take place after three months and then six-monthly. This review must be extended to include the child's specific clinical needs, for example, is health information up to date?

- *The Carer's Review* – should address whether the carer's training is up to date and whether they are happy to continue to look after the child.

What happens if a child dies in the care of a support carer?

Services need to have clear procedures which are known to carers, staff and parents about what should happen if a child dies while in the care of a support carer. These procedures should not just be about the mechanics but also about support services available to carers. A booklet produced by the National Foster Care Association (NFCA), *Death of children in foster care*, offers some useful advice (1996).

Resource issues

There are clearly financial implications for social services and health authorities who are organising family-based short-term care for children with complex healthcare needs. As a collaborative approach is needed, one option would be joint-funded posts for training, assessment and cooperation of joint procedures, practice guidelines and so on. This is advocated in the government's response to the Health Committee:

Joint planning and funding between health, social and education services is required, especially in respect of the care of children who have a chronic health problem or disability. (DoH, 1997)

Sufficient human resources need to be made available to support the training, assessment and coordination of these protocols.

Insurance and indemnity

Joint protocols or policies will also need to include information about insurance cover and liability. Authorities or agencies will be required to demonstrate that carers have received adequate training by appropriately trained health professionals. Health professionals providing this training should ensure that they are indemnified by the appropriate NHS body.

Support carers should be provided with insurance cover against claims for negligence resulting from invasive clinical treatment. This can either be by means of a placing agency's liability policy or alternatively from the NFCA's block policy available to local authorities and private agencies.

The NFCA policy has sums assured available from £1m to £5m and cover is conditional on details of likely treatment and procedures being supplied to the insurers such that a suitable endorsement can be prepared relating to the range of treatments given. This can either be on an individual case basis or alternatively by means of a policy statement detailing the specialist care to be performed by carers.

Conclusions

Children with complex healthcare needs are a rapidly growing group using family-based short-term care services. These children may require ongoing treatment for the rest of their lives and hospitalisation is not only inappropriate but costly.

The guidelines offered in this document are underpinned by the principle of children's rights. Under the legislation the local authority has a responsibility to provide a range of services and support for disabled children and their families which are designed to minimise the effects of disability and give them the opportunity to lead lives which are 'as normal as possible'. Where children can be cared for within a family setting, this must be the most appropriate option.

This has placed new demands not only on support carers but on all agencies including the local authorities arranging the provision. Issues around training and liability have provided particular challenges.

If, however, family-based short-term carers are to provide care to children who require clinical treatments they need appropriate training and insurance cover. This will involve a collaborative approach between health and social services where expertise is pooled and responsibilities are clearly defined.

This report has outlined some of the areas that a multiagency group would need to consider when drawing up a local policy. Following these guidelines will mean that the risks to children and support carers are minimised and will allow children to receive care in an ordinary setting.

References

City of York Council (1997) Community Services Children's Division, supplementary procedures for the Sharing (Health) Care.

DoH (1991) *The welfare of children and young people in hospital*, London: HMSO.

DoH (Department of Health) (1997) *Government response to the reports of the Health Committee on health services for children and young people*, Session 1996-97: 'The specific health needs of children and young people in the community, home and school' (314-1); 'Hospital services for children and young people' (128-1); 'Child and adolescent mental health services' (26-1), London: HMSO.

Disability Discrimination Act (1995) *Goods and services*, London: RADAR.

Nutritional Care Team (1994a) *Gastrostomy feeding and you*, Birmingham: The Children's Hospital, Ladywood, Middleway.

Nutritional Care Team (1994b) *Tube feeding and you*, Birmingham: The Children's Hospital, Ladywood, Middleway.

NFCA (National Foster Care Association) (1996) *Death of children in foster care. Making it work*, London: NFCA.

Rhodes, A., Lenehan, C. and Morrison, J. (1997) *Supporting disabled children who need invasive clinical procedures. A guide to good practice for Barnardos Family Support Services*, London: Barnardos.

Russell, P. (1996) 'Managing the risks', in H. Platt, J. Hughes, C. Lenehan, S. Morris and M. Flynn, *We miss her when she goes away*, Manchester: National Development Team.

Servian, R. (1996) *Policy for the management of medicines and Life Saving Procedures*, Dudley Social Services Direct Care.

United Nations Convention on the Rights of the Child (1989) Act.

Appendix A:
Sample healthcare plan

Name of child ....

Date of birth ....

Address ....

....

Telephone number ....

Name of carer ....

Address ....

....

Telephone number ....

Contact information ....

Family contact I ....   Family contact 2 ....

Name ....   Name ....

Tel No (work) ....   Tel No (work) ....

      (home) ....   (home) ....

Relationship ....   Relationship ....

Clinic/hospital treatment.......................   GP ....

Name ....   Name ....

Tel No ....   Tel No ....

Describe the medical condition or specific healthcare need and give details of the child's individual symptoms and needs.

Daily care requirements (eg, at lunchtime):

Clinical procedures which need to be administered – by whom; under what conditions; when and how?

Identify training which will need to be provided:

Who will need to be trained?

Training to be provided by:

Describe what constitutes an emergency for the child, and what action to take if this occurs:

Who is responsible in an emergency? (see emergency plan):

Healthcare plan agreed by: (give signatures)

Healthcare professional: ....

Parent: ....

Child: ....

Scheme coordinator: ....

Carer: ....

[This form has been taken from a set of sample forms in Rhodes et al (1997).]

Appendix B:
Parental consent form

Parental agreement on general administration of medication

Request to supervise the administration of medicines to my child.

1)   I confirm that my child ....
requires the following medicines to be taken in accordance with medical advice and as detailed in the
healthcare plan.

Medicines	Where stored (eg, fridge)	Time required	Amount	How given

2)   Names of carers authorised to give medication   ....

3)   Please indicate which of the following you would like the support carer to carry out by ticking one box:

a)   Keep the medicines and assist my child who will take the medication him/herself
as detailed above.   ☐

b)   Keep the medicine and supervise my child to ensure that he/she takes the medicines
as detailed above.   ☐

c)   Keep the medicines only and seek professional assistance in administering them.   ☐

If appropriate, please state which professionals will assist: ....

In making this request I accept full responsibility for my child's welfare.

I agree that all medicines will be given to the carer in the original container.

Signed (Parent) ....   Date..

Decision by carer
(please delete as appropriate)

1)   I am willing/not willing to meet your request

2)   I agree to establish a written record of action taken.   Yes/No

3)   I agree to make arrangements for the storage of the medicine.   Yes/No

4)   I agree to undergo training to give the above medication.   Yes/No

Signed (Carer) .... Date ....

Signed (for Social Services) .... Date ....

This consent form could be adapted to include specific clinical procedures, for example

Type of procedure ....

For how long will your child need this to be undertaken ....

(Please state if not known)

Method ....

Timing ....

Side-effects ....

Procedures to take in an emergency ....

In making this request I accept full responsibility for my child's welfare and consent to the carer carrying out the above healthcare procedure for my child.

Signed .... Date ....
(Parent)

Decision by carer
(please delete as appropriate)

1)   I am willing/not willing to meet your request

2)   I agree to establish a written record of action taken.   Yes/No

3)   I agree to undergo training to administer the above procedure.   Yes/No

4)   After appropriate training I agree to administer the above   Yes/No
     healthcare procedure.

Signed (Carer) .... Date ....

Signed (for Social Services) .... Date ....

[Adapted from sample forms used by Dudley Social Services, Servian (1996).]

Appendix C:
Form and guidance for the life-saving administration of medicines and completed example form

(i) Guidance on drawing up a protocol for emergency procedures

The document outlined should be completed in respect of each child where emergency or other irregular procedures may be required. Guidance is provided under each section of the form.

Each case will be different and will require individual procedures which will need to be communicated to all carers in contact with the child. When formulating an emergency procedure, regard should be given to the availability of those who can administer the medication, the age of the child, the layout of the household, the timescale for administering medication and all other potential problems that could be encountered in any emergency.

Full name of child/young person ....

Date of birth ....

Address ....

....

Telephone No ....

Background

In this section give a detailed description of the child's health needs, including a medical history summary, symptoms and likely consequences of no action being taken. Provide name of GP and consultant and any advice they have provided.

Treatment

In this section give an outline of the treatment to be administered and who specifically is to be involved in giving it. If invasive procedures such as injections are required, support carers must be trained. Provide details of symptoms and a step-by-step procedure for action in the event of an emergency. Include in this section the names of the trained carers, and who is to do what in an emergency. Note also parents/carers and others who are to be notified, eg. scheme coordinator. If paramedic team is to be called it may be appropriate to have a letter from GP/consultant regarding the child's condition for their use.

Training

This section should give details of the training received by the named carers mentioned above, as well as dates of courses, including refresher courses.

Note: Appropriate training should be arranged via relevant healthcare professional (who will confirm by letter the level and extent of training given).

Location of emergency medicines

Specify in this section where medication is stored (two locations) and where spares are stored. Emphasise that medication should not be locked in a cupboard. Specify who is responsible for checking on a daily/ weekly//monthly basis that medication is not out of date and how these checks are recorded.

Specify also the procedure for obtaining fresh medication and who is responsible for ensuring that medication is available, eg, parents. Some children may also carry the necessary medicine for use in an emergency when staff are not available. This will need to be agreed with parents and detailed here.

Response to emergency incidents

In this section clearly set out in detail what to do in case of emergency. State who is trained and where and when they can be contacted. It is very important that the procedure for emergency treatment is checked with the appropriate medical personnel and, when agreed, that a copy is sent to the social services department for information.

For example the procedure might state the following:

1) Carry out emergency procedure as trained.

2) (a) At the same time as (1) above, ensure someone urgently telephones the following people in the order given.

Telephone 999 requesting the attendance of a paramedic team and emphasising urgency

 (b) Telephone family doctor

 (c) Telephone parents

 (d) Telephone named medical contact

 (e) Telephone family link/shared care scheme.

3) Stay with child until professional help arrives.

4) Debriefing session to take place for all involved convened by social services staff.

Note: The first priority in each case must be to administer medication and call for a paramedic ambulance.

Other factors for consideration and additional procedures

List here any precautionary measures that need to take place and/or any preventative actions. It is important if a child has a life threatening illness that support carers are aware of the potential dangers and that he/she can be observed virtually all the time. Precautionary measures could therefore include:

A watchful eye to be kept on .... at all times.

He/she should be accompanied to the toilet.

All support carers involved to be reminded frequently about procedures and who to send for in the event of an attack.

Frequent reminders to be given to children and parents about the need for cooperation in keeping certain products away from the child if the child is allergic to them.

Mention should be made of all aspects of the child's care about which support carers should know.

Key people

List key contact people.

These procedures should be reviewed each year and when the child moves to new carers, etc.

A copy of these notes should be placed in an easily accessible place and checked at each review.

It will be the responsibility of the parent (or delegated person[s]) to acquaint the support carer with the contents of this document.

The procedures should be signed by the relevant parties, dated and a review date documented. For example:

I agree that these are the appropriate procedures to be undertaken in such an emergency as outlined above.

Mr/Ms/Mrs/Miss .... Parent (where main advocate)..

Dr .... GP or appropriate other medical advisor ....

We have read and understood these procedures.

Support carer .... Date ....

Scheme coordinator .... Date ....

Review date ....

[Adapted from sample forms used by Dudley Social Services, Servian (1996).]

(ii) Completed example form

Emergency procedures in the event of a need for administration of medicines

The following is an example of the form outlined in Appendix C (i) which has been completed for a child with severe allergies and asthma. It is an example of one child's situation where two carers are always available. Names have been changed.

Emergency procedure for:

Name	Date of birth	Address
Jade Roberts	19.12.88	23 Downs Road Westbrook

Jade's mother – Stella Roberts

Jade's short-term carers – Kate and Lesley Day. Kate is the main carer and has been trained to administer medication and give life-saving treatment.

Kate has received training from Dr Graham to:

- recognise a severe allergic reaction;

- carry out the administration of the medication;

- administer intramuscular adrenaline;

- perform Cardio-Pulmonary Resuscitation.

Background

Jade is highly allergic to a wide variety of substances, particularly foods. Jade's most severe allergies are to dairy products, eg, milk and cheese, but she is also allergic to fish, meat, wheat, oats, dogs, birds, some fruit, nuts, washing-up liquid, some jewellery, wool and possibly also grass. A strong reaction may occur when such substances are either inhaled or ingested or come into contact with her skin. The allergic reactions range from swelling of her lips and a rash, through to asthma attacks and unconsciousness.

Although Jade has a good idea of which substances cause an allergic response, there are times when a new allergy suddenly arises and it is then not immediately clear what substance is causing it.

Jade receives treatment from Mr Obaidullah, Consultant Paediatrician at Westbrook Hospital. He confirms that Jade has been followed up in his clinic with multiple food allergies, for which she is on a special diet. He also makes the point that she also has chest symptoms which can develop on to acute bronchospasm. For Jade's asthma attacks, she uses inhalers and a nebuliser.

Jade is on a special diet, excluding eggs, cheese, milk, meat and fish various cereals and nuts. It is necessary for her to carry/wear at all times a medicalert bracelet identifying that she suffers from multiple allergies.

Outline of treatment

Treatment of an allergic reaction includes, where possible, removing her from the responsible agent, assisting her to use her inhaler and, if necessary, giving an injection of adrenaline intramuscularly as trained. In this situation it will be necessary to dial 999, call for an ambulance and contact her mother (Stella Roberts) or other nominated contact. Cardio-Pulmonary Resuscitation from trained carer (Kate Day) may also be required.

Responding to incidents

In the event of an allergic reaction being evident, eg, red lumps which are usually swollen, large red blotches, or a red rim around her mouth, wheezing or vomiting, the following procedures will apply:

Action	To be taken by
• Remove Jade from the possible source of the reaction	Kate or Lesley
• Irrigate the affected area with clear water	Kate
• Where appropriate assist Jade to use her inhaler	Kate
• At the onset of any reaction, Jade's mum, (Stella Roberts) or her appoind nominees (grandmother/uncle) will be contacted by telephone and asked to attend immediately	Kate or Lesley

Stella Roberts has indicated that she or her appointed nominees (grandmother/aunt) could get to Kate and Lesley's house within 20 minutes.

Any further treatment needed must await instructions from Stella or her nominees on their arrival.

However, in the event of a whole body reaction or severe asthma attack, emergency procedures would be followed.

Procedure in the event of a need for emergency treatment

Action	To be taken by
• Telephone 999 requesting the attendance of a paramedic team for a child suffering a possible life threatening allergic reaction.	Lesley
• Remain with Jade until the paramedic team arrive.	Kate or Lesley
• Check for pulse and breathing.	Kate
• Give Cardio-Pulmonary Resuscitation as trained if necessary.	Kate
• Give injection of adrenaline intramuscularly as trained if necessary. An epipen with a dose of ...mg would be used to administer the injection.	Kate
• If still having difficulty breathing 10 minutes after first injection, repeat injection.	Kate
• Inform the scheme coordinator.	Kate/Lesley
• Stay with Jade until professional help arrives.	Kate/Lesley
• When paramedic team arrives give them a copy of Dr ...'s letter dated .... This letter is to be kept in an envelope pinned on the notice board by the phone next to the numbers for emergency contacts (as above) and this form.	Kate/Lesley

Location of treatment

- Two Epipens containing the measured dose of adrenaline will be kept in the first aid box.

- Jade's volumatic inhaler will be kept in the same location.

- **Treatment must be available at all times and so should not be kept in a locked cupboard.**

- Kate Day will check weekly that both sets of Epipens are available and will also check the expiry date. Kate is responsible for liaising with Stella regarding expiry date of medication and Stella is responsible for supplying new medication.

- It is Stella's responsibility to ensure that the treatment needed for Jade is available at all times.

Training

Injection administration is to be carried out by Kate who has received the appropriate medical training from Dr Graham.

Kate will also carry out the administration of the medication. Kate has undergone training and been given a letter of attendance. She has been trained to recognise a severe allergic reaction, how to administer intramuscular adrenaline and how to perform Cardio-Pulmonary Resuscitation. Copies of Kate's letter of attendance should be kept on file at the scheme.

Jade's parents, grandmother, and aunt and Kate and Lesley Day will all have a copy of these procedures and they will be brought to the attention of any one who comes into contact with Jade.

Refresher training courses will be given at regular intervals.

Key people

.... (Stella Roberts, address and telephone no)

.... (Grandmother, address and telephone no)

.... (Aunt, address and telephone no)

.... Scheme coordinator

.... Dr Ng (GP)

Additional procedures

It is important that carers are aware of the possible areas of high risk.

Jade should use her own soap and towel.

If Jade has a wound only water should be applied.

If Kate and Lesley's children are drinking orange juice or milk they will be separated to avoid the risk of accidental splashing.

Kate and Lesley's children will be informed and given regular reminders that Jade should not be given anything to eat, eg, sweets.

Frequent reminders will be given to the children about the need for cooperation in keeping certain products away from Jade.

Kate and Lesley will log all incidents which occur, however minor. A log will also be kept of Jade's experiences during her stay to assist her mother in the event of a delayed reaction.

Kate or Lesley will notify Stella of anything that has occurred out of the ordinary during the day. This information will be relayed orally but must also be written in the log which will be sent home daily with Jade and returned by her mum when she next stays.

Any new experiences, eg, cookery, farm visits, need to be discussed in advance with Stella to arrange their management.

Outside play – it will be necessary to watch out for other children giving Jade snacks and sweets.

Kate, Lesley and their children should be aware that the following could cause an allergic reaction:

Water   Jade should not use bubble bath, washing-up liquid, washing powder, fabric conditioners or soap.

Scissors   Jade is to use only plastic scissors.

Materials   100% wool is not to be used but synthetic fabrics are fine.

Cooking   Jade can only participate when ingredients have been checked with her mother.

Dressing up   Jade must not have any metal jewellery or any 100% woollen items.

The procedures in this document must be discussed each year at the annual review and before if there are any changes in circumstances.

A copy will be kept by the scheme and a copy given to each carer.

This procedure is dated ....

Date for review ....

Signed (Parent) ....

Signed (Carer/s) ....

Signed (Scheme coordinator) ....

Signed (GP or appropriate other medical advisor) ....

[Adapted from sample forms used by Dudley Social Services, Servian (1996).]

Appendix D:
Recording training

(i) Record of training given to implement clinical procedure

Brief description of clinical procedure

Nature of training to be given

Who is to provide training?

Names of carer/s to be trained

Dates of training

Has the training been satisfactory?   Yes/No

Signed (Carers) ....

(Printed name) ....

Signed (Trainer) ....

(Printed name and status) ....

I agree that the above clinical procedure and training are appropriate to the needs of my patient.

Mr/Mrs/Ms (full name of patient) ....

Signed .... GP or appropriate medical officer

Name and status of medical officer ....

[Adapted from sample forms used by Dudley Social Services, Servian (1996).]

(ii) Record of updates and new training

Training and dates	Signed (name and status)
Please clearly state what training covers professional assessed as able to give	Must be signed by medical advisor/ training.

[Adapted from sample forms used by Dudley Social Services, Servian (1996).]

Appendix E:
Record of administration
of medication

Child's name ....

Date	Medicine and dose	Method of administration	Time given	Any reactions	Name	Signature

[Adapted from sample forms used by Dudley Social Services, Servian (1996).]

Appendix F:
Example of written guidelines for complex care procedures

Note: This is a general protocol which would need to be modified for each child's specific needs.

Gastrostomy feeding

A gastrostomy is a direct opening through the abdominal wall into the stomach. A gastrostomy tube allows liquid feed to be delivered directly into the stomach.

Many disabled children have feeding problems as a result of central nervous system damage, and a gastrostomy tube ensures that the child receives an adequate nutritional intake.

Gastrostomy feeds can be given as a bolus feed (ie, a specified amount of liquid feed) over 30 minutes; or as a continuous feed via a pump; or as a combination of both. The method chosen will be the one that best meets the need of the child.

Equipment

1. Adapter and feeding tubing

2. Syringe or feeding bag

3. Feeding solution and/or medication

4. Water to flush tubing.

Procedure

1. Wash hands.

2. Gather equipment together.

3. Using the syringe, withdraw a small amount of fluid and check with litmus paper. The paper should turn pink.

4. Attach the adapter and feeding tube to a syringe or bag.

5. Fill the syringe or feeding bag and tubing with feed; this prevents large amounts of air from entering the stomach, and causing distension and discomfort.

6. Open the safety plug of the gastrostomy and attach the tubing and adapter. The child should be positioned on their side with their head elevated.

7. Elevate the feed bag or syringe and using gravity, let the feed flow in. A pump is used for continuous feeds which are normally overnight.

8. When the feed is complete, flush the feeding tube and gastrostomy tube with at least 10mls of water.

9. Disconnect the feeding tube and adapter from the gastrostomy and close the safety plug.

10. Wash the equipment and hands.

Medications an be given as above. Some may require dilution with water if they are thick. Give the medicines before or after the feed.

Do not mix into the total amount of feed to be given

The gastrostomy site should be cleaned with mild soap and water one or twice a day. If the gastrostomy is a button type this can be rotated to help prevent the skin underneath breaking down.

Problems	Solutions
1) Gastrostomy site infection	1) Prevent by good hygiene. Seek medical advice to treat.
2) Vomiting	2) Stop feed initially. Attach large empty syringe and extension tubing to gastrostomy tube. Lower the syringe.
3) Leakage	3) Assess for sign of infection to site, treat if present.
	Attach large empty syringe and extension tubing to the gastrostomy tube. The raised intra-gastric pressure will be reduced as the feed comes up into the tubing. This feed will then re-enter the stomach when gastric emptying permits.
4) Bleeding	4) Reassure. This should stop. If not, seek advice.
5) Tube blockage	5) Try a change to the child's position, or move feeding tube higher. Clear with cola or pineapple juice.

Prepared by Jill Igoe: Nursing Coordinator for Sharing (Health) Care – York.

Appendix G:
An example of a multiagency approach to organising services in York

City of York Council
Community Services Children's Division
Supplementary procedures for the Sharing (Health) Care Service

Introduction

These procedures should be read in conjunction with the Sharing Care Policy and Procedures Document. They are intended to provide a supplementary framework for the extension of the Sharing Care scheme to children who have specialist health needs over and above those catered for within the Sharing Care Scheme. The extension of the scheme is operated in partnership with the North Yorkshire Health Authority and York Health Services Trust, and will be overseen by a steering group of appropriate officers from the partner agencies.

These procedures will address the following areas:

- responsibilities of the health authority and health trust;

- responsibilities of the City of York;

- evaluation and monitoring of the scheme;

- eligibility criteria for children using the scheme;

- placement of children;

- approval of carers;

- training and support of carers;

- administration of medication and performance of 'nursing' tasks;

- medical emergencies and the death of a child in placement.

Section One: Responsibilities of the partner authorities

Role of the health authority

The health authority will be responsible for the funding of payments to carers at a rate of £30 per overnight stay and £15 for day care for children placed through the scheme. The health authority will indicate at the beginning of each financial year the level of funding and consequent number of placements available to the City of York.

The health authority will identify an appropriate person to act as a member of the steering group for the scheme. That person will contribute to the monitoring and evaluation of the scheme.

The health authority will commission a nursing coordinator and appropriate 'out of hours' support for carers for the scheme from the York Health Services Trust. Out of hours support will be commissioned from the York Health Services Trust and will include telephone access to qualified nursing staff for carers.

The health authority will ensure that all GPs have received general information about the scheme and that they have been made aware of the potential implications of children requiring medical attention while in support carers' homes.

Role of the York Health Services Trust

The York Health Services Trust will identify an appropriate manager to represent the Trust on the steering group. The role of the manager will be to contribute to the management and evaluation of the scheme with particular reference to the function of the nursing coordinator and the 'out of hours' support to carers.

The York Health Services Trust will appoint an appropriately qualified person to act as nursing coordinator for the scheme. That person would normally be a registered nurse with significant experience of working with children with disabilities requiring 'nursing' care.

The York Health Trust will make arrangements for the 'out of hours' support for carers. This will involve carers having telephone access to the nursing staff on the paediatric ward.

Role of the City of York Community Services Department

The City of York will identify an appropriate officer to act as a member of the steering group and to contribute towards the monitoring and evaluation of the scheme.

The City of York will be responsible for the day-to-day management of the scheme.

The City of York will ensure that it has staff to recruit, assess and support carers for the scheme.

The City of York will provide the funding for Sharing Care payments to carers. Rates of fees will be published at the start of each financial year, and the authority will make clear the number of placements it intends to fund.

The City of York will make arrangements for the 'out of hours' support of carers for all circumstances other than support concerning the 'nursing' care of the child.

Section Two: Evaluation and monitoring of the scheme

During the period of the pilot project (October 1996 to March 1998) the partner agencies will arrange for the scheme to be externally evaluated. The evaluation process will include analysis of the following areas:

- the views of parents and children using the service on its effectiveness and capacity to meet their needs;

- the views of carers on the adequacy of training and support, and the appropriateness of placements;

- the views of placing social workers on the quality and effectiveness of the service;

- the views of the nursing coordinator and family placement officer on the effectiveness of the service;

- the views of other interested professionals, for example, paediatricians on the value added by the service extension;

- value for money, and the ability of the scheme to meet targets identified.

The evaluation will also consider the language and terminology used by the scheme in terms of its accessibility to families and carers, and the effectiveness of publicity and information, and will analyse unmet need, including the needs of those children who cannot be accommodated by the service.

The steering group of the partner agencies will meet at least every three months to consider the progress of the scheme in terms similar to those described above.

The steering group will ensure that it establishes an appropriate forum for parents and children to express their views on the progress of the scheme, by identifying either a parent representative for the steering group or a reference group.

Section Three: Placement of children

Eligibility criteria

The extension of the Sharing Care scheme will be available for children who have an ongoing physical or learning disability and who have additional health needs. These additional health needs will normally require the use of specific 'nursing' procedures with the child, for example:

- gastrostomy feeds;
- administration of oxygen;
- tracheostomy;
- suction of excretions from mouth/nose;
- management of poorly controlled fits.

It should be noted that, as care will be provided by carers who are not necessarily nursing qualified and provided in the carer's own home, there may be some children whose needs are such that the scheme will be unable to accommodate them, for example, children who require resuscitation via intubation and bagging on a regular basis.

Placement of children

Placements will be made in accordance with Section Two of the Sharing Care Procedures.

Parents and children will be invited to meet with the nursing coordinator to discuss their needs to assist in the process of identifying the best carer for the child. The nursing coordinator may request permission to discuss the child's needs with their paediatrician.

Once a potential carer has been identified and introduced to the parents the nursing coordinator will visit the parents and the child to discuss the specific details of how they prefer procedures to be performed. Parents and children will be requested to give individual consent for each of the 'nursing' procedures needed for the proper care of their child.

Section Four: Approval, training and support of carers

Recruitment and assessment of carers

All carers will be approved in accordance with the provisions of Section One of the Sharing Care Procedures.

Recruitment and advertising materials for the Sharing Care service will incorporate information about the need for carers who are able to offer care to children with additional health needs.

The nursing coordinator will undertake an initial visit with the family placement officer where potential carers express an interest in caring for children with additional health needs.

Preparation courses will include input from the nursing coordinator on children's health needs and the additional practical skills that may be needed by carers, and in conjunction with the family placement officers will discuss the emotional impact of caring for a child with significant health needs.

Applicants will be asked to indicate an interest in caring for children with additional health needs on their application form.

Once an application has been received all applicants will be assessed within the guidelines produced by BAAF. This will include the family placement officer and nursing coordinator undertaking a number of interviews with applicants in their own homes, both individually and as a couple where appropriate.

The nursing coordinator will assess the applicant's basic awareness of the needs of children with additional health needs and their capacity to undertake the tasks required. In conjunction with the family placement officer the nursing coordinator will also assess the applicant's motivation and emotional capacity to undertake the care of a child with additional health needs.

The nursing coordinator and family placement officer will prepare a joint report on these specific aspects separate to the Form F report, including a recommendation as to the suitability of the applicant to undertake this care. The report will be shared with the applicants but will not be submitted to the panel. It will be submitted to an appropriately qualified medical advisor, usually a paediatrician who will comment on the applicant's suitability and submit a recommendation to the Approval Panel.

The Panel will be invited to consider the approval of the applicants taking account of the comments of the medical advisor described above. If the Panel recommends approval the application will be submitted to the Agency decision maker with the supplementary report and the medical advisor's comments.

Matching and linking

The nursing coordinator will be involved in the process of identifying potential 'matches' between carers and children having knowledge of both the child's 'nursing' needs and the carers' capacities to meet those needs.

The nursing coordinator will accompany the family placement officer on visits to carers to discuss a potential link. The coordinator will ensure that carers are fully aware of the implications for them in meeting the child's health needs and that they are given accurate information on the 'nursing' procedures required.

The nursing coordinator may accompany the family placement officer and social worker on visits to parents and children to introduce potential carers if it would be considered helpful by the parents. The role of the coordinator would be to answer questions on the capacity of the carers to meet the child's health needs and the training and support carers would be offered in this respect.

Training of carers

Once a potential link has been identified, the nursing coordinator with the carers will identify an appropriate training programme to ensure that the carer is competent and confident with all the procedures needed to care for the child.

The nursing coordinator will ensure that carers have written information on each procedure and have been assessed as competent.

Carers may request additional training at any time. Refresher training in the administration of rectal diazepam and in complex procedures will be provided at six monthly intervals.

Support for carers

Carers will have an identified link worker as described in Section One of the Sharing Care Procedures. In addition they will have regular contact with the nursing coordinator at an interval negotiated between the carer and the coordinator, or if specific advice and support is needed in respect of a nursing procedure.

Outside of normal office hours, carers will have access to the Emergency Duty Team in respect of concerns for all matters relating to the child's welfare, except those relating to the 'nursing' needs of the child. Carers will have telephone access to the registered nurse on the paediatric ward at York District Hospital for advice and support in relation to the nursing procedures needed by the child. The paediatric ward will not give diagnoses or deal with emergencies. The latter should be dealt with by reference to the appropriate procedure below.

Section Five: Health considerations

Administration of medication and performance of nursing procedures

The service will have regard to the Invasive Procedures Policy and the provisions of the Sharing Care Procedures.

Carers will be expected to undertake such 'nursing' procedures as are necessary for the child's care and that are deemed reasonable by the nursing coordinator in consultation with the child's parents and paediatrician. This may include the following:

• management of gastrostomy feeds;

• management of tracheostomies;

• administration of oxygen;

• suction;

• management of poorly controlled fits;

• other procedures for which carers have received training and been deemed competent.

Carers will be expected to undertake training and reach a minimum standard of competence. They will be entitled to expect support and training from the nursing coordinator. Training may be commissioned by the nursing coordinator from an appropriately qualified health professional.

Carers will receive written information on all procedures they are asked to undertake.

It will be the responsibility of parents to ensure that their child has all medication needed for the duration of the placement. Medications must be supplied in the original packaging with the child's name and pharmacist's instructions clearly visible. Carers must ensure that they consult with parents about the child's medication to ensure that they are aware of any changes.

Carers must keep an accurate written record of all medication given and procedures performed. They will be supplied with standard drug record forms. Carers must ensure that they have accurate written information about the medication, dosage and procedures needed by the child.

Carers will be able to contact either the nursing coordinator or the paediatric ward at York District Hospital should they need advice about a 'nursing procedure'.

Parents will be asked to give consent for each 'nursing' procedure undertaken and for the administration of medications.

Medical emergencies

Carers and parents will agree prior to the placement the circumstances in which parents want to be contacted if their child is unwell. In all circumstances of a child requiring admission to hospital, parents will be informed immediately by the carer. If the child's parents are not available the carer will contact the person named by the parent prior to the placement as the emergency contact.

In the event of a child requiring medical attention, except for emergency treatment, carers will in the first instance contact their GP to visit the child. Parents will be informed of the GP visit and of any treatment undertaken. Carers will ensure that they make available to GPs such written information as they have about the child's health needs, including drug record sheets where appropriate.

Carers will contact the emergency services if, in their judgement, the child requires emergency treatment. This would include circumstances such as unusual fitting, unusual or no response to medication, and respiratory failure. All carers will receive training in emergency first aid and on procedures for dealing with a medical emergency.

Section Six: Death of a child

Action to be taken by carers

In the tragic circumstances of a child dying in the carer's home the carer shall immediately contact the GP, and either the family placement officer or the emergency duty team.

Carers will inform the family placement officer or emergency duty team if a child dies following admission to hospital from the carer's address.

Carers should expect the relevant health and community services officers to ensure that all appropriate procedures are followed.

Support for carers

Carers will be visited either by the family placement officer or the emergency duty team as soon as is practicable following notification. The officer concerned should ensure that the carer receives immediate support by way of counselling, transport, or any other appropriate immediate action.

Carers will be offered bereavement counselling which will be arranged by the community services department.

Action to be taken by the service manager and family placement officer

On receiving notification from the carer the family placement officer or emergency duty team will inform the service manager or duty service manager, and make arrangements to visit the carers.

If the parents of the child are not already present the service manager will visit them at home, or make appropriate arrangements for them to be contacted (eg, arrange with another local authority if the parents are away from home). The service manager will inform the social worker for the child and ensure that appropriate arrangements are put into place to support the family.

If the parents of the child are present, the service manager will ensure that the parents are contacted either by the service manager or the child's social worker and that they are offered appropriate support.

The service manager will ensure that the assistant director for children's services is informed. If the child has been placed by another local authority the service manager will ensure that the relevant senior manager is informed.

Action to be taken by the City of York

The City of York will ensure that the requirements of the 1989 Children Act Schedule 2 Paragraph 20 are met. The appropriate senior officer will notify the Secretary of State through the Social Services Inspectorate, and the North Yorkshire Health Authority.

There will be a management review of the circumstances of the child's death within 30 days. The purpose of this review will be to:

* ensure that appropriate procedures have been followed;

* ensure that appropriate support arrangements have been made for parents and carers;

* make recommendations if any changes to the arrangements are required.

The review will consider the implications of any post mortem undertaken.

If the post mortem indicates any suspicious circumstances surrounding the child's death, the City of York will ensure that a review under the arrangements of 'Working Together: Part 8' are considered.

Every effort must be made to minimise the distress caused to parents and carers, to avoid delay in reaching any conclusions, and to keep them informed of the progress of the review.

Appendix H: Feedback form

In order to help us improve any subsequent editions of this report, please could you complete this form.

Have you found this document useful?

Which parts have you used most?

Which parts did you find least useful?

What would you like to see included in updated documents?

What is Shared Care Network?

Shared Care Network is the umbrella organisation for hundreds of family-based short-term care services in England and Northern Ireland. Shared Care Network supports these services by:

*   offering an information service;

*   lobbying to promote appropriate services;

*   organising conferences and training;

*   promoting the rights of carers and their families;

*   encouraging good practice.

Other titles from Shared Care Network

Stronger links

A practical guide to good practice for children's family-based short-term care services. The guide will be of use to purchasers of services, schemes in the process of setting up and established schemes who will be able to reflect and measure their existing practice against the good practice offered. Temporarily out of print at time of writing (October 1998).

New horizons

A practical guide to organising family-based short breaks for people with autism, which will be especially useful for professionals working in shared care services, parents of people with autism and carers offering breaks to people with autism.

A question of quality

Questionnaires and guidelines for telephone surveys of parents' and link carers' views on family-based short-term care services for children.

After careful consideration

A booklet designed for panel members who assess the suitability of foster carers intending to offer short breaks to disabled children. It contains important information on the purpose and functions of a panel, roles and responsibilities and the differences between family-based short-term care and foster care. Studies are used to help readers consider a variety of issues that may arise.

Quality counts

Family-based short-term care has been one of the great success stories over the past 20 years in the support of disabled people and their families. But how can those involved in local schemes make sure that they are providing the highest possible standards of service? *Quality counts* is the result of practical research carried out by Shared Care Network which looked at simple methods of consulting parents, support carers and disabled service users on the quality of their local schemes.

For further details or an order form, contact Shared Care Network, The Norah Fry Research Centre, 3 Priory Road, Bristol, BS8 1TX. Tel: 0117 928 9814. Fax: 0117 946 6553.